FIRST STEPS IN ORIGAMI

Origami Playtime

Belinda Webster

PowerKiDS press

Published in 2020 by **The Rosen Publishing Group, Inc.**
29 East 21st Street, New York, NY 10010

Cataloging-in-Publication Data

Names: Webster, Belinda.
Title: Origami playtime / Belinda Webster.
Description: New York : PowerKids Press, 2020. | Series: First steps in origami | Includes glossary and index.
Identifiers: ISBN 9781725314962 (pbk.) | ISBN 9781725314986 (library bound) | ISBN 9781725314979 (6 pack)
Subjects: LCSH: Origami--Juvenile literature. | Paper art--Juvenile literature.
Classification: LCC TT872.5 B437 2020 | DDC 736.982--dc23

Manufactured in the United States of America

CPSIA Compliance Information: Batch CSPK20: For Further Information contact Rosen Publishing, New York, New York at 1-800-237-9932.

CONTENTS

WHAT IS ORIGAMI?

Origami is the craft of paper folding, invented in Japan hundreds of years ago. The word "origami" means "folded paper" in Japanese.

Origami paper is thin but strong, so it can be folded many times.

It is square and is usually white on one side.

You could use ordinary scrap paper instead of origami paper, but make sure it's not too thick.

BASIC FOLDS

To follow the steps in this book, there are three basic folds you need to learn.

VALLEY FOLD

To make a valley fold, fold the paper up on itself so that the crease is at the bottom, like a valley. A valley fold will be shown by a dashed line, like this.

MOUNTAIN FOLD

To make a mountain fold, fold the paper the other way, away from you. You want the crease to point up, like the peak of a mountain. We use a dotted line to show a mountain fold.

STEP FOLD

A step fold is a mountain fold and a valley fold next to each other.

1 First, make a valley fold by folding the paper up on itself so the crease is at the bottom.

2 Now unfold.

3 Next, make a mountain fold above the valley fold you have just made.

4 Push the mountain fold over the valley fold and press it flat. You now have a step fold.

KEY

- - - - - Valley fold

.... Mountain fold

Step fold

Direction to move paper

PUSH Direction to push (or pull, etc.)

WINDMILL

Blow on this windmill to watch it spin, or stand it outside and wait for the breeze to make it turn.

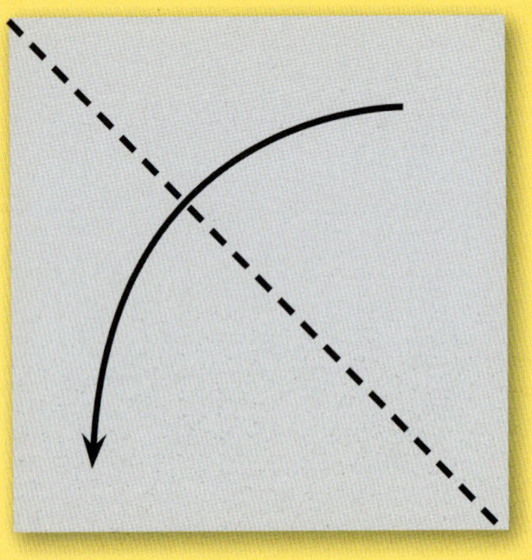

1 Start with the paper white side up, like this. Valley fold it in half, as shown. Unfold.

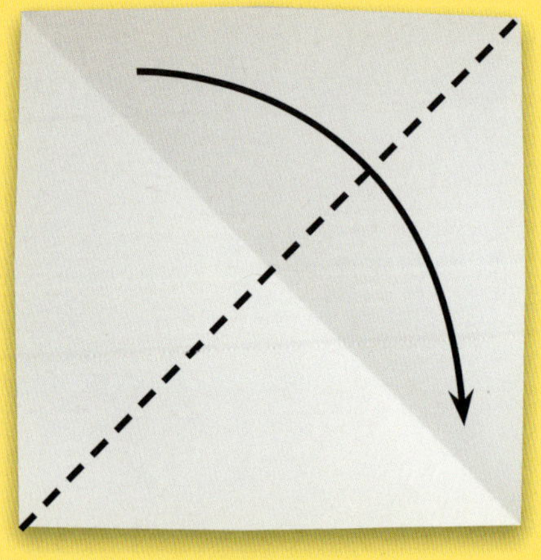

2 Valley fold the paper in half the other way. Unfold.

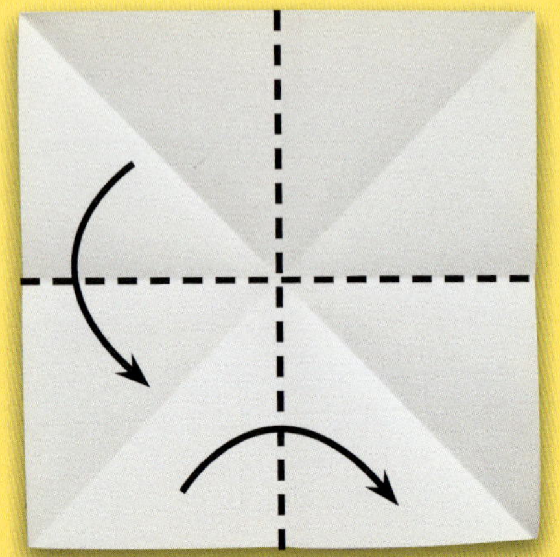

3 Valley fold the paper from top to bottom and unfold it. Then valley fold it from left to right. Unfold.

4 Your paper should now look like this.

5 Valley fold the left and right sides in, so they meet in the middle.

6 Valley fold the top edge in to the middle. Crease well, then unfold.

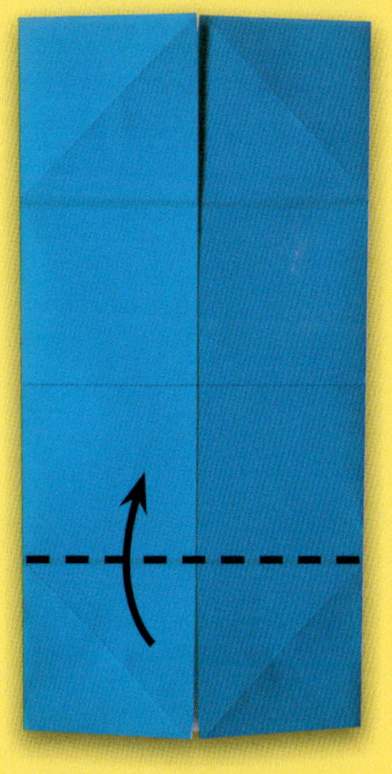

7 Valley fold the bottom edge in to the middle. Crease well, then unfold.

8 Valley fold the top layer of the top left and right flaps out to the sides, as shown. This will pull the paper behind upward.

9 Your model should look like this. Pull the top flap down so that it lies flat.

10 Valley fold the top layer of the bottom left and right flaps out to the sides, as shown.

11 Your model should look like this. Pull the bottom flap up so that it lies flat.

12 Valley fold the bottom left flap down.

13 Valley fold the top right flap up.

14 Ask an adult to help you use a tack to attach your windmill to a pencil so that you can hold it or stand it up. Blow gently on the windmill to see it turn.

STAR

This origami model looks tricky, but it's really easy once you get the hang of it. You'll need six pieces of paper to create one star.

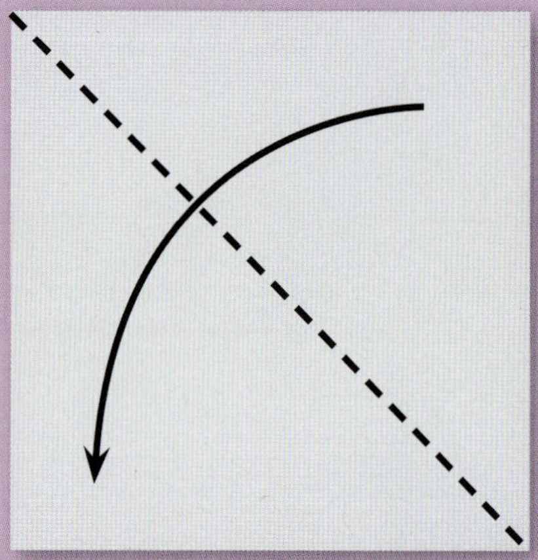

1 Start with one piece of paper white side up, like this. Valley fold it in half, as shown. Unfold.

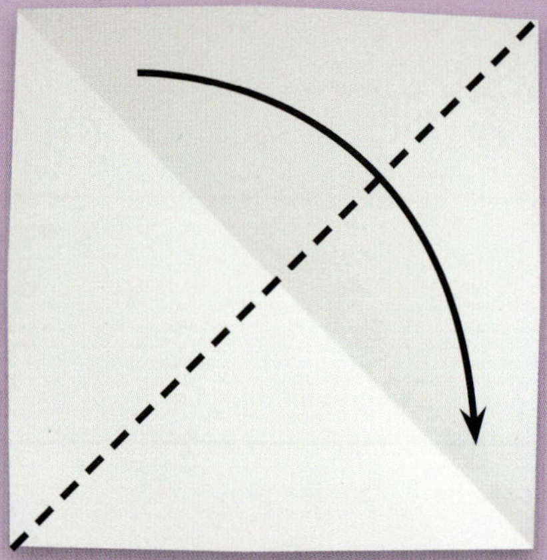

2 Valley fold the paper in half the other way, then unfold.

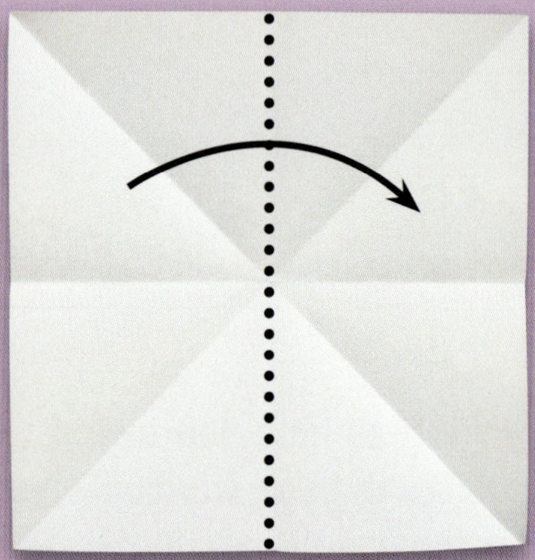

3 Mountain fold the paper from left to right. Unfold.

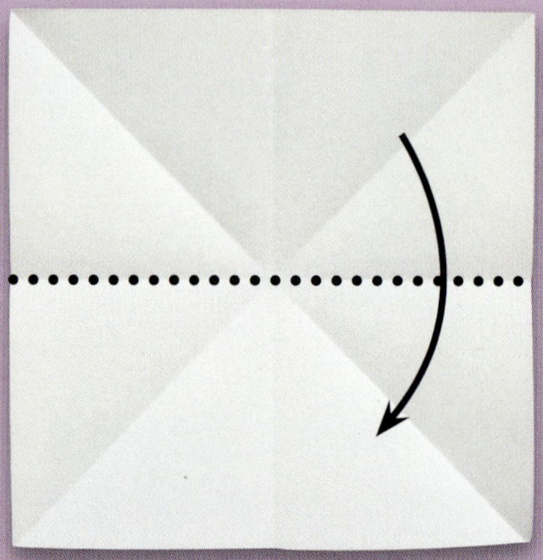

4 Mountain fold from top to bottom, then unfold.

5 Push the two outer edges inward to meet each other.

6 The paper will fold in on itself to make triangle shape. Press it down flat.

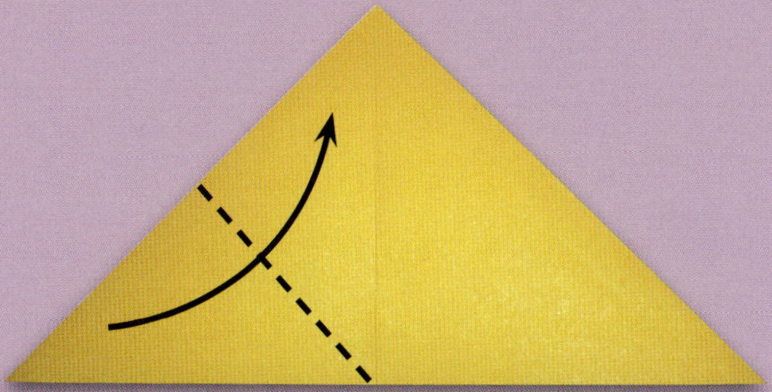

7 Valley fold the top layer of the left point to meet the top point. Crease well and unfold.

8 Valley fold the top layer of the right point to meet the top point. Crease well and unfold.

9 Turn over the paper. Repeat steps 7 and 8.

10 Create five more triangle shapes, by repeating steps 1 to 9. Once you have six in total, you can start creating your star.

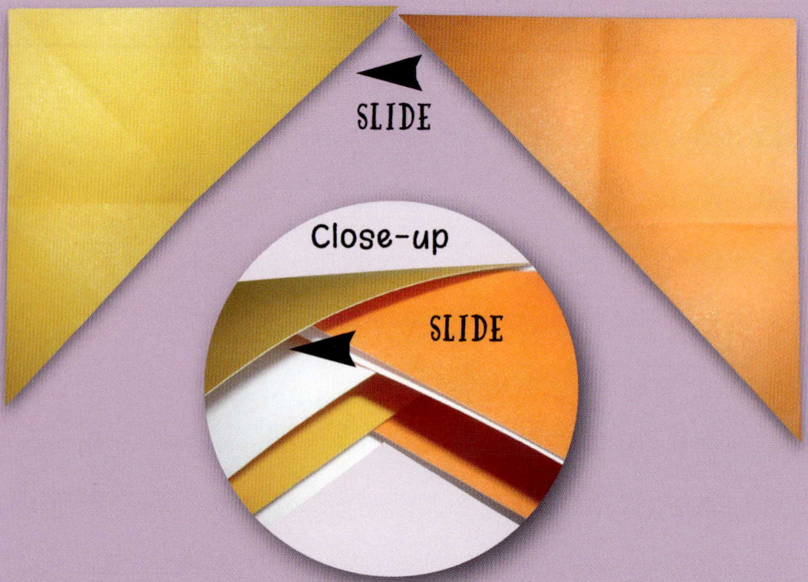

11 Start with two triangles. Slide the left points of the right triangle into the top pockets of the other triangle, as shown. Slide the points in as far as they will go.

12 Your paper should now look like this. Pull the middle crease toward you to open up the top. Pinch the two top corners to shape your star.

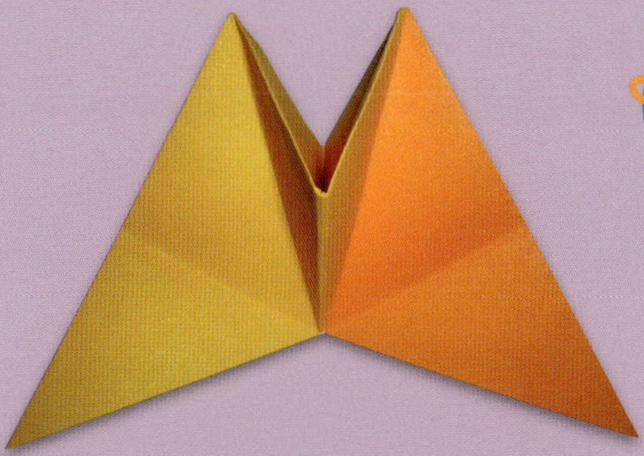

13 Your paper should now look like this.

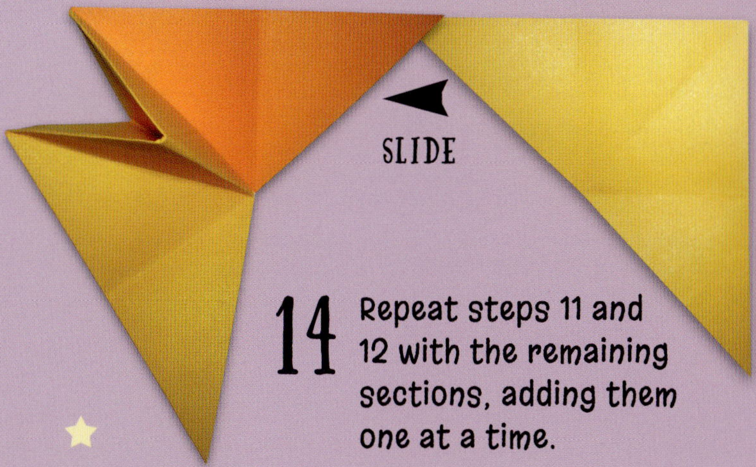

14 Repeat steps 11 and 12 with the remaining sections, adding them one at a time.

15 Finish your star by slotting the last section into the first section and repeating step 12. Your star is now complete!

JUMPING FROG

This little leaper is easy to make. Make two, and have a frog race with a friend!

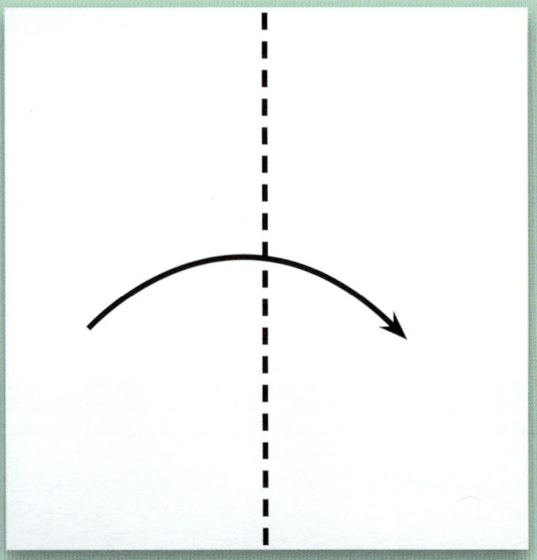

1 Start with a square of paper white side up, like this. Valley fold it in half from left to right.

2 Valley fold the top right corner, as shown. Crease well and unfold.

3 Valley fold the top left corner, as shown. Crease well and unfold.

4 Mountain fold the top section where the two creases cross over. Unfold.

5 Collapse the top section by pushing the sides together and toward you.

6 Your model should look like this. Push the top edge down to flatten it into a triangle.

7 Valley fold the left and right sides of the top triangle up to create your frog's front legs.

8 Valley fold the bottom square in half from bottom to top.

9 Valley fold the top flap down, just below halfway, as shown.

10 Valley fold up once more, as shown.

11 Turn over your frog. This is what it should look like.

12 To make your frog jump, push down on its back and release.

GIVE YOUR FROGGY FRIEND SOME EYES SO IT CAN SEE WHERE IT'S GOING!

CHOMPING DINO

Someone's hungry! Follow the steps to create your very own munching beast. Let's hope he's not a meat eater!

1 Start with the paper white side up, like this. Valley fold it in half from left to right, then unfold.

2 Valley fold the left section to meet the middle crease.

3 Do the same on the other side.

4 Rotate the paper so the top is now the bottom.

5 Valley fold the left corner over to meet the middle crease.

6 Do the same on the other side.

7 Valley fold the paper in half from bottom to top.

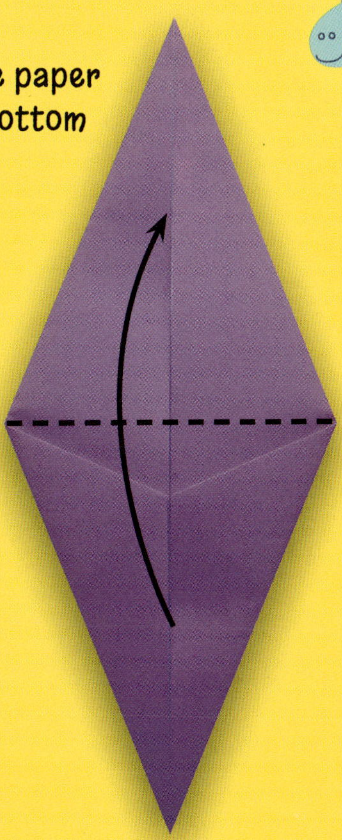

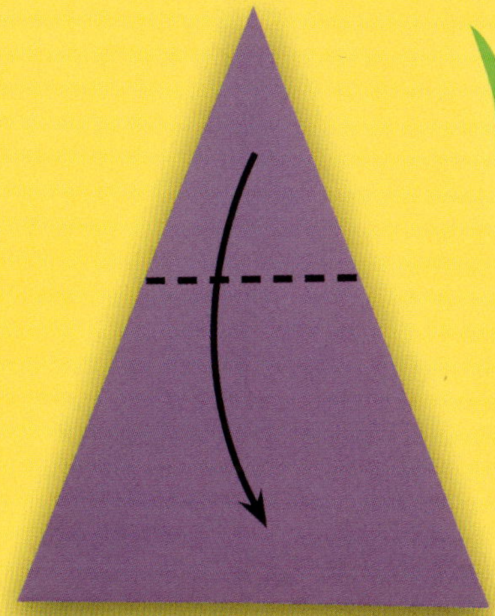

8 Valley fold the top layer down, as shown, so the point meets the bottom edge.

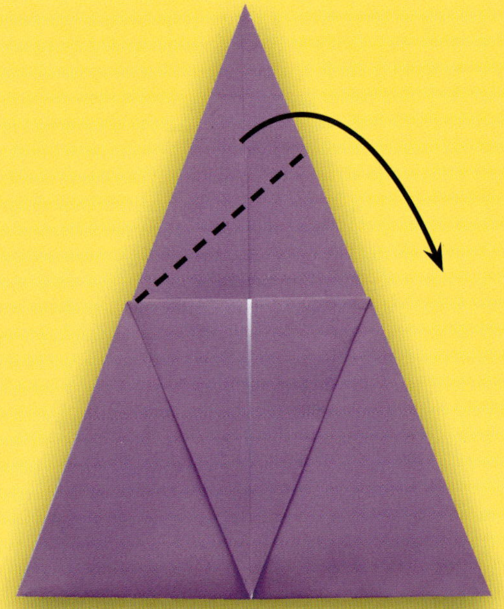

9 Valley fold the top point over to the right, like this.

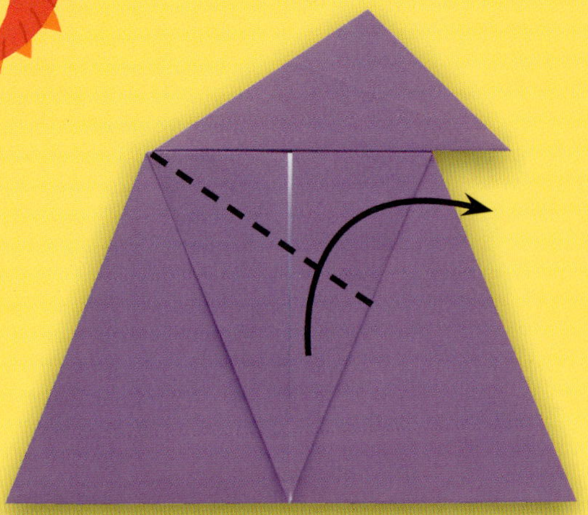

10 Valley fold the bottom flap up and to the right.

11 Valley fold the top point down to where the flaps meet, using the crease you made earlier as a guide.

12 Press down well, then unfold.

13 Now unfold the fold you made in step 9.

14 Your paper should look like this. Tuck the right edge in, as shown, along the crease lines you have already made.

15 Your paper should start to look like this. Keep tucking in the side and press it down flat to make a triangle.

16 Valley fold the bottom flap, as shown, using the crease you made earlier as a guide.

17 Press down firmly, then unfold.

18 Now unfold the fold you made in step 10.

19 Repeat step 14 on this flap, tucking the right edge in. Use the crease lines you made earlier to help.

20 Press down the paper to flatten it into a triangle. This is your dino's head.

21 Mountain fold, as shown, to create the neck.

22 To make your dino snap its jaws, open and close the back of the neck.

GLOSSARY

crease A line made by a fold.

mountain fold A fold where the crease points up at you, like a mountain.

rotate To turn in a circular movement.

step fold A fold that creates a zigzag, or step, in the paper.

valley fold A fold where the crease points away from you, like a valley.

windmill A building that makes energy using the wind.

INDEX